To

_____

FROM

_____

The quoted ideas expressed in this book (but not scripture verses) are not, in all cases, exact quotations, as some have been edited for clarity and brevity. In all cases, the author has attempted to maintain the speaker's original intent. In some cases, quoted material for this book was obtained from secondary sources, primarily print media. While every effort was made to ensure the accuracy of these sources, the accuracy cannot be guaranteed. For additions, deletions, corrections or clarifications in future editions of this text, please write BRIGHTON BOOKS.

Scripture quotations are taken from:

The Holy Bible, King James Version

The Holy Bible, New International Version (NIV) Copyright © 1973, 1978, 1984, by International Bible Society. Used by permission of Zondervan Publishing House. All rights reserved.

The Holy Bible, New King James Version (NKJV) Copyright © 1982 by Thomas Nelson, Inc. Used by permission.

The New American Standard Bible®, (NASB) Copyright © 1960, 1962, 1963, 1968, 1971, 1972, 1973, 1975, 1977, 1995 by The Lockman Foundation. Used by permission.

Holy Bible, New Living Translation, (NLT) Copyright © 1996. Used by permission of Tyndale House Publishers, Inc., Wheaton, Illinois 60189. All rights reserved.

New Century Version®. (NCV) Copyright © 1987, 1988, 1991 by Word Publishing, a division of Thomas Nelson, Inc. All rights reserved. Used by permission.

The Holman Christian Standard Bible™ (HCSB) Copyright © 1999, 2000, 2001 by Holman Bible Publishers. Used by permission.

Cover Design by Kim Russell / Wahoo Designs
Page Layout by Bart Dawson

ISBN 1-58334-226-5

Printed in the United States of America

table of contents

introduction

Because you are holding a book with the words "for graduates" on its cover, it is likely that congratulations are in order. If you're a recent graduate, please accept a hearty "Well done!" You've earned it.

As you begin the next phase of your life's journey, you'll be making lots of decisions; this book can help you decide wisely. This text contains 30 devotional readings intended to help you discover the plans that God has in store for you.

The ideas on these pages offer Biblically-based, time-tested principles for finding abundance, peace, and joy in the post-graduate world. This book can serve as an inspirational reminder of the opportunities and possibilities that await you in the days and years ahead.

God stands ready and willing to lead you along a path of His choosing. So today, if you do nothing else, begin the lifelong search for His direction: trust His wisdom, obey His commandments, and let His Son reign in your heart. When you do, you will have accepted a graduation gift that will change your life forever and endure throughout eternity.

AFTER GRADUATION...
NOW WHAT?

*You will show me the way of life, granting me the joy
of your presence and the pleasures of living with you forever.*

Psalm 16:11 NLT

N ow that school is a not-so-distant memory, you may be faced with a multitude of decisions: where to live, where to work, what to do about your personal relationships. And hopefully, you have also decided that graduation is just the beginning, not the end, of your spiritual and intellectual journey.

You may be asking yourself an important question: "What does God want me to do with my life?" It's an easy question to ask but, for many of us, a difficult question to answer. Why? Because God's purposes aren't always clear to us. Sometimes we wander aimlessly in a wilderness of our own making. And sometimes, we struggle mightily against God in a vain effort to find success and happiness through our own means, not His.

How can we know precisely what God's intentions are? The answer, of course, is that even the most well-intentioned believers face periods of uncertainty and doubt about the direction of their lives. So, too, will you.

When you arrive at one of life's crossroads, that is precisely the moment when you should turn your thoughts and prayers toward God. When you do, He will make Himself known to you in a time and manner of His choosing.

Are you earnestly seeking to discern God's purpose for your life? If so, this book is intended to remind you of several important facts: (1) God has a plan for your life. (2) If you seek that plan sincerely and prayerfully, you will find it. (3) When you discover God's purpose for your life, you will experience abundance, peace, joy, and power—God's power—the only kind of power that really matters.

ഔ Let your fellowship with the Father and with the Lord Jesus Christ have as its one aim and object a life of quiet, determined, unquestioning obedience.

Andrew Murray

ഔ Only God's chosen task for you will ultimately satisfy. Do not wait until it is too late to realize the privilege of serving Him in His chosen position for you.

Beth Moore

ഔ Life is too short and the world too compassion-starved for you to keep subsisting in situations that drag you down and curtail your potential to help advance the Kingdom. There's just too much at stake.

Bill Hybels

ഔ I have been all over the world, and I have never met anyone who regretted giving his or her life to Christ.

Billy Graham

ഔ The measure of a life, after all, is not its duration but its donation.

Corrie ten Boom

ဢ People, places, and things were never meant to give us life. God alone is the author of a fulfilling life.

Gary Smalley and John Trent

ဢ Life is not a problem to be solved; it is an adventure to be lived.

John Eldredge

ဢ A VERSE AND A PRAYER અ

For God is working in you, giving you the desire to obey him and the power to do what pleases him.

Philippians 2:13 NLT

Dear Lord, let me choose Your plans. You created me, and You have called me to do Your work here on earth. Today, I choose to seek Your will and to live it, knowing that when I trust in You, I am eternally blessed. ~Amen

YOUR JOURNEY WITH CHRIST

And when He had spoken this, He said to him,
"Follow Me."

John 21:19 NKJV

J esus loved you so much that He endured unspeakable humiliation and suffering for you. How will you respond to Christ's sacrifice? Will you take up His cross and follow Him (Luke 9:23), or will you choose another path? When you place your hopes squarely at the foot of the cross, when you place Jesus squarely at the center of your life, you will be blessed.

The 19th-century writer Hannah Whitall Smith observed, "The crucial question for each of us is this: What do you think of Jesus, and do you yet have a personal acquaintance with Him?" Indeed, the answer to that question determines the quality, the course, and the direction of our lives today and for all eternity.

The old familiar hymn begins, "What a friend we have in Jesus . . . ." No truer words were ever penned. Jesus is the sovereign Friend and ultimate Savior of mankind. Christ showed enduring love for His believers by willingly sacrificing His own life so that we might have eternal life. Now, it is our turn to become His friend.

Now that you've graduated, it's time to take the next step on your life's journey; make certain that you take that step with Christ by your side. Accept His love, obey His teachings, and share His message with your neighbors and with the world. When you do, you will demonstrate that your acquaintance with the Master is not a passing fancy; it is, instead, the cornerstone and the touchstone of your life.

෩ A believer comes to Christ; a disciple follows after Him.

Vance Havner

෩ It takes real faith to begin to live the life of heaven while still upon the earth, for this requires that we rise above the law of moral gravitation and bring to our everyday living the high wisdom of God. And since this wisdom is contrary to that of the world, conflict is bound to result. This, however, is a small price to pay for the inestimable privilege of following Christ.

A .W. Tozer

෩ Christ is not valued at all unless He is valued above all.

St. Augustine

෩ Christ is like a river that is continually flowing. There are always fresh supplies of water coming from the fountain-head, so that a man may live by it and be supplied with water all his life. So Christ is an ever-flowing fountain; He is continually supplying His people, and the fountain is not spent. They who live upon Christ may have fresh supplies from Him for all eternity; they may have an increase of blessedness that is new, and new still, and which never will come to an end.

Jonathan Edwards

∂ The love life of the Christian is a crucial battleground. There, if nowhere else, it will be determined who is Lord: the world, the self, and the devil—or the Lord Christ.

Elisabeth Elliot

∂ When an honest soul can get still before the living Christ, we can still hear Him say simply and clearly, "Love the Lord your God with all your heart and with all your soul and with all your mind . . . and love one another as I have loved you."

Gloria Gaither

∂ A VERSE AND A PRAYER ∂

And I am convinced that nothing can ever separate us
from his love. Whether we are high above the sky or
in the deepest ocean, nothing in all creation will ever
be able to separate us from the love of God
that is revealed in Christ Jesus our Lord.

Romans 8:38–39 NLT

Dear Lord, You sent Your Son so that I might have abundant life and eternal life. Thank You, Father, for my Savior, Christ Jesus. I will follow Him, honor Him, and share His Good News, this day and every day. ~Amen

WHY AM I HERE?

O LORD, you have examined my heart and know
everything about me. You know when I sit down or stand up.
You know my every thought when far away.
You chart the path ahead of me . . . .

Psalm 139:1-3 NLT

God has things He wants you to do and places He wants you to go. The most important decision of your life is, of course, your commitment to accept Jesus Christ as your personal Lord and Savior. And, once your eternal destiny is secured, you will undoubtedly ask yourself the question, "What now, Lord?" If you earnestly seek God's will for your life, you will find it . . . in time.

As you prayerfully consider God's path for your life, you should study His Word and be ever watchful for His signs. You should associate with fellow believers who will encourage your spiritual growth, and you should listen to that inner voice that speaks to you in the quiet moments of your daily devotionals.

As you continually seek God's purpose for your life, be patient: your Heavenly Father may not always reveal Himself as quickly as you would like. But rest assured: God is here, and He intends to use you in wonderful, unexpected ways. He desires to lead you along a path of His choosing. Your challenge is to watch, to listen . . . and to follow.

⁊ Every believer may be brought to understand that the only object of his life is to help to make Christ King on the earth.

Andrew Murray

⁊ We aren't just thrown on this earth like dice tossed across a table. We are lovingly placed here for a purpose.

Charles Swindoll

⁊ When God speaks to you through the Bible, prayer, circumstances, the church, or in some other way, He has a purpose in mind for your life.

Henry Blackaby and Claude King

⁊ Without God, life has no purpose, and without purpose, life has no meaning.

Rick Warren

⁊ We must focus on prayer as the main thrust to accomplish God's will and purpose on earth. The forces against us have never been greater, and this is the only way we can release God's power to become victorious.

John Maxwell

℺ If the Lord calls you, He will equip you for the task He wants you to fulfill.

Warren Wiersbe

℺ We are most vulnerable to the piercing winds of doubt when we distance ourselves from the mission and fellowship to which Christ has called us.

Joni Eareckson Tada

℺ A VERSE AND A PRAYER ℞

I urge you to live a life worthy of the calling you have received.

Ephesians 4:1 NIV

Dear Lord, let Your purposes be my purposes. Let Your priorities be my priorities. Let Your will be my will. Let Your Word be my guide. And, let me grow in faith and in wisdom today and every day. ~Amen

THE PATH... ACCORDING TO GOD

Psalm 37 teaches us that, "The steps of the godly are directed by God. He delights in every detail of their lives" (vv. 22 NLT). In other words, God is intensely interested in each of us, and He will guide our steps *if* we serve Him obediently.

When we sincerely offer heartfelt prayers to our Heavenly Father, He will give direction and meaning to our lives—*but* He won't force us to follow Him. To the contrary, God has given us the free will to follow His commandments . . . or not.

When we stray from God's commandments, we invite bitter consequences. But, when we follow His commandments, and when we genuinely and humbly seek His will, He touches our hearts and leads us on the path of His choosing.

Will you trust God to guide *your* steps? You should. When you entrust your life to Him completely and without reservation, God will give you the strength to meet any challenge, the courage to face any trial, and the wisdom to live in His righteousness and in His peace. So trust Him today and seek His guidance. When you do, your next step will be the right one.

Ⓢ Make my path sure, O Lord. Establish my goings. Send me when and where You will and manifest to all that Thou art my guide.

Jim Elliot

Ⓢ Are you serious about wanting God's guidance to become a personal reality in your life? The first step is to tell God that you know you can't manage your own life, that you need His help.

Catherine Marshall

Ⓢ If we want to hear God's voice, we must surrender our minds and hearts to Him.

Billy Graham

Ⓢ Only He can guide you to invest your life in worthwhile ways. This guidance will come as you "walk" with Him and listen to Him.

Henry Blackaby and Claude King

Ⓢ God does not furnish us with a detailed road map. When we are with Him, we may not always know whither, but we know with whom.

Vance Havner

∾ God never leads us astray. He knows exactly where He's taking us. Our job is to obey.

Charles Swindoll

∾ It's a bit like river rafting with an experienced guide. You may begin to panic when the guide steers you straight into a steep waterfall, especially if another course appears much safer. Yet, after you've emerged from the swirling depths and wiped the spray from your eyes, you see that just beyond the seemingly "safe" route was a series of jagged rocks. Your guide knew what he was doing after all.

Shirley Dobson

∾ A VERSE AND A PRAYER ⇒

The LORD is good and does what is right;
he shows the proper path to those who go astray.

Psalm 25:8 NLT

Lord, let Your will be my will. When I am confused, give me maturity and wisdom. When I am worried, give me courage and strength. Let me be Your faithful servant, Father, always seeking Your guidance and Your will for my life. ~Amen

A DAILY JOURNEY OF PRAYER AND MEDITATION

Watch ye therefore, and pray always . . . .
Luke 21:36 KJV

Once you finally discover God's purpose for your life, your search will be over and your life will be complete . . . right? Wrong! Your search to discover the unfolding of God's plan for your life is not a destination to be reached; it is a path to be traveled, a journey that unfolds day by day. And, that's exactly how often you should seek direction from your Creator: one day at a time, without exception.

Daily prayer and meditation are a matter of will and habit. You must willingly organize your time by carving out quiet moments with God, and you must form the habit of daily worship. When you do, you'll discover that no time is more precious than the silent moments you spend with your Heavenly Father.

Is prayer an integral part of your daily life, or is it a hit-or-miss routine? Do you "pray without ceasing," or do you simply cease praying? Do you pray throughout the day, or do you bow your head only when others are watching?

The quality of your spiritual life will be in direct proportion to the quality of your prayer life. Prayer changes things, and it changes you. Today, instead of turning things over in your mind, turn them over to God in prayer. Instead of worrying about your next decision, ask God to lead the way. Don't limit your prayers to meals or to bedtime; pray constantly. God is listening; He wants to hear from you; and *you* most certainly need to hear from Him.

🔊 The remedy for distractions is the same now as it was in earlier and simpler times: prayer, meditation, and the cultivation of the inner life.

A. W. Tozer

🔊 As you pray, ask God to give you this day a single mind, a submissive mind, a spiritual mind, and a secure mind.

Warren Wiersbe

🔊 Prayer is not a vending machine which spits out the appropriate reward. It is a call to a loving God to relate to us.

Philip Yancey and Tim Stafford

🔊 When you pray, things may remain the same, but you begin to be different.

Oswald Chambers

🔊 God knows that we, with our limited vision, don't even know that for which we should pray. When we entrust our requests to Him, we trust Him to honor our prayers with holy judgment.

Max Lucado

ॐ Pray, and let God worry.

Martin Luther

ॐ Are you weak? Weary? Confused? Troubled? Pressured? How is your relationship with God? Is it held in its place of priority? I believe the greater the pressure, the greater your need for time alone with Him.

Kay Arthur

ॐ A Verse and a Prayer ∽

Do not be anxious about anything, but in everything,
by prayer and petition, with thanksgiving,
present your requests to God.

Philippians 4:6 NIV

Dear Lord, I will open my heart to You. I will take my concerns, my fears, my plans, and my hopes to You in prayer. And, then, I will trust the answers that You give. You are my loving Father, and I will accept Your will for my life today and every day that I live. ~Amen

Extreme Demands and High Expectations

*Obviously, I'm not trying to be a people pleaser!
No, I am trying to please God. If I were still trying
to please people, I would not be Christ's servant.*

Galatians 1:10 NLT

As a citizen of the 21ˢᵗ century, you know that the demands of everyday life can be high, and expectations even higher. The media delivers an endless stream of messages that tell you how to look, how to behave, how to eat, and how to dress. The media's expectations are impossible to meet—God's are not. God doesn't expect you to be perfect, and neither should you.

The difference between perfectionism and realistic expectations is the difference between a life of frustration and a life of contentment. Only one earthly being ever lived life to perfection, and He was the Son of God. The rest of us have fallen short of God's standard and need to be accepting of our own limitations and the limitations of others.

If you find yourself frustrated by the unrealistic demands of others (or by unrealistic pressures of the self-imposed variety), it's time to ask yourself whom you're trying to impress, and why.

If you're trying to impress your friends, or if you're trying to imitate the appearance of some Hollywood celebrity, it's time to reconsider your priorities. Your first responsibility is to the Heavenly Father who created you and to the Son who saved you. Then, you bear a powerful responsibility to be true *to yourself*. And, of course, you owe debts of gratitude to friends and family members. But, when it comes to meeting society's unrealistic expectations, forget it!

If you become discouraged with your inability to be perfect, remember that when you accepted Christ as your Savior, God accepted you for all eternity. Now, it's your turn to accept *yourself*. When you do, you'll feel a tremendous weight being lifted from your shoulders. After all, pleasing God is simply a matter of obeying His commandments and accepting His Son. But as for pleasing everybody else? *That's* impossible!

 ℮ Make God's will the focus of your life day by day. If you seek to please Him and Him alone, you'll find yourself satisfied with life.

Kay Arthur

 ℮ Too many Christians have geared their program to please, to entertain, and to gain favor from this world. We are concerned with how much, instead of how little, like this age we can become.

Billy Graham

 ℮ Fashion is an enduring testimony to the fact that we live quite consciously before the eyes of others.

John Eldredge

ஓ Some day we will stand before God. And when we do, we will need something more than speculative imagination or a warm, fuzzy feeling.

Charles Swindoll

ஓ Get ready for God to show you not only His pleasure but His approval.

Joni Eareckson Tada

ஓ A VERSE AND A PRAYER ଔ

So then each of us shall give account of himself to God.
Romans 14:12 NKJV

Lord, help me to live up to *Your* expectations not *the world's* expectations. Let me seek Your will and follow Your path not a path that is chosen for me by others. Your way is the right path for me. And when I follow You, Father, I will better serve my family, my friends, my neighbors, and the world. ~Amen

CELEBRATING THE JOURNEY

Rejoice in the Lord always. I will say it again: Rejoice!
Philippians 4:4 HCSB

G raduation day is a day of celebration, but what about all the other days? That's an easy question to answer: Today, tomorrow, and every day after that should be a time for celebration as we consider the Good News of God's free gift: salvation through Jesus Christ.

For devout believers, every day begins and ends with God and His Son. Christ came to this earth to give us abundant life and eternal salvation. We say "thank you" to our Maker when we treasure each day. Thus, we should use our time here on earth to serve God, to celebrate His marvelous gifts, and to share His Good News with the world.

What do you expect from the day ahead? Are you expecting God to do wonderful things, or are you living beneath a cloud of apprehension and doubt? The familiar words of Psalm 118:24 remind us of a profound yet simple truth: "This is the day which the LORD hath made" (KJV). Our duty, as believers, is to rejoice in God's marvelous creation.

As you prepare for the exciting days ahead, take time to pause and thank God for His gifts. And then demonstrate your gratitude by *celebrating* His creation, His blessings, and His love.

🕚 Praise and thank God for who He is and for what He has done for you.

Billy Graham

🕚 There is no division into sacred and secular; it is all one great, glorious life.

Oswald Chambers

🕚 Your life is not a boring stretch of highway. It's a straight line to heaven. And just look at the fields ripening along the way. Look at the tenacity and endurance. Look at the grains of righteousness. You'll have quite a crop at harvest . . . so don't give up!

Joni Eareckson Tada

🕚 Wherever you are, be all there. Live to the hilt every situation you believe to be the will of God.

Jim Elliot

🕚 Christ and joy go together.

E. Stanley Jones

§ Now is the only time worth having because, indeed, it is the only time we have.

C. H. Spurgeon

§ With each new dawn, life delivers a package to your front door, rings your doorbell, and runs.

Charles Swindoll

§ A VERSE AND A PRAYER ©

This is the day which the LORD has made;
let us rejoice and be glad in it.

Psalm 118:24 NASB

Lord, Your desire is that I be complete in Your joy. Joy begets celebration. Today, I celebrate the life and work You have given me, and I celebrate the lives of my friends and family. Thank You, Father, for Your love, for Your blessings, and for Your joy. Let me treasure Your gifts and share them this day and forever. ~Amen

TRUSTING GOD'S DIRECTION

Therefore, whether we are at home or away, we make it
our aim to be pleasing to Him. For we must all appear
before the judgment seat of Christ, so that each
may be repaid for what he has done in the body,
whether good or bad.

2 Corinthians 5:9–10 HCSB

God has things He wants to tell us, and He's hard at work trying to get His message through; unfortunately, many of us are too busy, too distracted, or too stubborn to listen. So instead of discovering God's direction, we may wander aimlessly, searching for the abundant life, but never finding it.

If you choose to wander aimlessly through this life, nobody can stop you. But if you sincerely seek to discover God's purpose (and experience His abundance), here are seven things that you can do:

1. Carve out time for daily prayer, meditation, and Bible study: even a few minutes each day can make a big difference in your life.

2. Attend worship services regularly and be a contributing member of your fellowship: fellow Christians will help you become a better Christian.

3. Choose friends who encourage you to do the right thing. Avoid those who tempt you to do otherwise.

4. Seek the wisdom of mentors, trusted friends, and family members. Don't be too stubborn to accept their advice.

5. Be watchful for signs: remember that sometimes God's messages are subtle.

6. Listen to your conscience, and pay attention to the quiet voice that speaks to you when you genuinely open your heart to God.

7. If at first you don't succeed, don't allow yourself to become discouraged. Instead, keep trusting God and keep seeking His direction until you find it . . . and rest assured: you *will* find it.

ಉ We can prove our faith by our commitment to it and in no other way. Any belief that does not command the one who holds it is not a real belief—it is only a pseudo-belief.

A. W. Tozer

ಉ It may be that the day of judgment will dawn tomorrow; in that case, we shall gladly stop working for a better tomorrow. But not before.

Dietrich Bonhoeffer

ಉ Our lives, we are told, are but fleeting at best, like roses they fade and decay; then let us do good while the present is ours, be useful as long as we stay.

Fanny Crosby

ಉ Faith never asks whether good works are to be done, but has done them before there is time to ask the question, and it is always doing them.

Martin Luther

ಉ A spiritual gift is a manifestation of God at work through you. God works in and through you to bear fruit. The focus is on God and what He does through you.

Henry Blackaby and Claude King

❧ God will help us become the people we are meant to be, if only we will ask Him.

Hannah Whitall Smith

❧ When you ask God to do something, don't ask timidly; put your whole heart into it.

Marie T. Freeman

❧ A VERSE AND A PRAYER ❧

Ask, and it will be given to you; seek, and you will find; knock, and it will be opened to you. For everyone who asks receives, and he who seeks finds, and to him who knocks it will be opened.

Matthew 7:7-8 NKJV

Dear Lord, I am Your creation, and You created me for a reason. Give me the wisdom to follow Your direction and perfect will for my life's journey. Lead me, Father, and let me trust You completely, today and forever. ~Amen

CHOOSING YOUR FRIENDS, CHOOSING YOUR BEHAVIORS

Whoever walks with the wise will become wise;
whoever walks with fools will suffer harm.

Proverbs 13:20 NLT

Some friendships help us honor God; these friendships should be nurtured. Other friendships place us in situations where we are tempted to dishonor God by disobeying His commandments; friendships that dishonor God have the potential to do us great harm.

Because we tend to become like our friends, we must choose our friends carefully. Because our friends influence us in ways that are both subtle and powerful, we must ensure that our friendships are pleasing to God. When we spend our days in the presence of godly believers, we are blessed not only by those friends but also by our Creator.

Do you seek to live a life that is pleasing to God? If so, you should build friendships that are pleasing to Him. When you do, your Heavenly Father will bless you and your friends with gifts that are simply too numerous to count.

🙠 Do you want to be wise? Choose wise friends.

Charles Swindoll

🙠 Though I know intellectually how vulnerable I am to pride and power, I am the last one to know when I succumb to their seduction. That's why spiritual Lone Rangers are so dangerous—and why we must depend on trusted brothers and sisters who love us enough to tell us the truth.

Chuck Colson

🙠 The best times in life are made a thousand times better when shared with a dear friend.

Luci Swindoll

🙠 Perhaps the greatest treasure on earth and one of the only things that will survive this life is human relationships: old friends. We are indeed rich if we have friends. Friends who have loved us through the problems and heartaches of life. Deep, true, joyful friendships. Life is too short and eternity too long to live without old friends.

Gloria Gaither

ℬ Is any pleasure on earth as great as a circle of Christian friends by a good fire?

C. S. Lewis

ℬ Be united with other Christians. A wall with loose bricks is not good. The bricks must be cemented together.

Corrie ten Boom

ℬ A VERSE AND A PRAYER ℭ

Do not be misled: "Bad company corrupts good character."
1 Corinthians 15:33 NIV

Lord, You seek abundance and joy for me and for all Your children. One way that I can share Your joy is through the gift of friendship. Help me to be a loyal friend. Let me be ready to listen, ready to encourage, and ready to offer a helping hand. Keep me mindful that I am a servant of Your Son Jesus. Let me be a worthy servant, Lord, and a worthy friend. And, let the love of Jesus shine through me today and forever. ~Amen

DOING YOUR WORK, DISCOVERING YOUR MISSION

*Whatever you do, work at it with all your heart,
as working for the Lord, not for men.*

Colossians 3:23 NIV

God has work for you to do, but He won't make you do it. Ever since the days of Adam and Eve, God has allowed His children to make choices for themselves, and so it is with you. You have choices to make . . . lots of them. If you choose wisely, you'll be rewarded; if you choose unwisely, you'll suffer the consequences.

Whether you're in school or in the workplace, your success will depend, in large part, upon the quality and quantity of your work. God has created a world in which diligence is rewarded and sloth is not. So whatever you choose to do, do it with commitment, excitement, and vigor.

God did not create you for a life of mediocrity; He created you for far greater things. Reaching for greater things usually requires work and lots of it, which is perfectly fine with God. After all, He knows that you're up to the task, and He has big plans for you . . . very big plans.

The world does not consider labor a blessing; therefore it flees and hates it, but the pious who fear the Lord labor with a ready and cheerful heart, for they know God's command, and they acknowledge His calling.

Martin Luther

I seem to have been led, little by little, toward my work; and I believe that the same fact will appear in the life of anyone who will cultivate such powers as God has given him and then go on, bravely, quietly, but persistently, doing such work as comes to his hands.

Fanny Crosby

We are expected to use all available means. We are not allowed to be idle and do nothing simply because we say we are trusting in Providence.

C. H. Spurgeon

Do noble things, do not dream them all day long.

Charles Kingsley

Let us not be content to wait and see what will happen, but give us the determination to make the right things happen.

Peter Marshall

∞ Let us not cease to do the utmost, that we may incessantly go forward in the way of the Lord; and let us not despair of the smallness of our accomplishments.

John Calvin

∞ Keep adding, keep walking, keep advancing; do not stop, do not turn back, do not turn from the straight road.

St. Augustine

∞ A VERSE AND A PRAYER ∞

I do not consider myself yet to have taken hold of it.
But one thing I do: Forgetting what is behind and straining
toward what is ahead, I press on toward the goal to win
the prize for which God has called me
heavenward in Christ Jesus.

Philippians 3:13-14 NIV

Dear Lord, make my work pleasing to You. Help me to sow the seeds of Your abundance everywhere I go. Let me be diligent in all my undertakings and give me patience to wait for Your harvest. ~Amen

DISCOVERING THE POWER OF FAITH

> *But Jesus beheld them, and said unto them,*
> *"With men this is impossible;*
> *but with God all things are possible."*
> Matthew 19:26 KJV

As you move on to the next phase of your life, you'll encounter sunny days and cloudy ones. When the sun is shining and all is well, you'll find it easy to have faith in God's plan. But, when your life takes an unexpected turn for the worse, as it will from time to time, your faith will be tested. In times of trouble and doubt, God remains faithful to you. You, in turn, should be faithful to Him.

Occasional disappointments are an inevitable part of every life, including yours. Such setbacks are simply the price that all of us must sometimes pay for our willingness to take risks as we follow our dreams. But even when we encounter bitter disappointments *today*, we must never lose hope in the promise of a better *tomorrow*.

Jesus taught His disciples that if they had faith, they could move mountains. You can too. When you place your faith, your trust, indeed your life, in the hands of Jesus, you'll be amazed at the marvelous things He can do with you and through you. So strengthen your faith through praise, through worship, through Bible study, and through prayer. And trust God's plans. With Him, all things are possible, and He stands ready to open a world of possibilities to you—in happy times *and* in tough times—*if* you have faith.

🔊 The measure of faith must always determine the measure of power and of blessing. Faith can only live by feeding on what is Divine, on God Himself.

Andrew Murray

🔊 Faith sees the invisible, believes the unbelievable, and receives the impossible.

Corrie ten Boom

🔊 Shout the shout of faith. Nothing can withstand the triumphant faith that links itself to omnipotence. For "this is the victory that overcometh the world." The secret of all successful living lies in this shout of faith.

Hannah Whitall Smith

🔊 God specializes in things thought impossible.

Catherine Marshall

🔊 When it is a question of God's almighty Spirit, never say, "I can't."

Oswald Chambers

∞ Faith in faith is pointless. Faith in a living, active God moves mountains.

Beth Moore

∞ Only God can move mountains, but faith and prayer can move God.

E. M. Bounds

∞ A VERSE AND A PRAYER ∞

*I tell you the truth, if you have faith as small as
a mustard seed, you can say to this mountain,
"Move from here to there" and it will move.
Nothing will be impossible for you.*

Matthew 17:20 NIV

Dear God, sometimes this world can be a fearful place, full of uncertainty and doubt. In those dark moments, help me to remember that You are always near and that You can overcome any challenge. Give me faith and let me remember always that with Your love and Your power, I can live courageously and faithfully today and every day. ~Amen

BEYOND OUR DOUBTS

*When doubts filled my mind,
your comfort gave me renewed hope and cheer.*

Psalm 94:19 NLT

Even the most faithful Christians are overcome by occasional bouts of fear and doubt. You are no different. When you feel that your faith is being tested to its limits, seek the comfort and assurance of the One who sent His Son as a sacrifice for you.

Have you ever felt your faith in God slipping away? If so, you are not alone. Every life—including yours—is a series of successes and failures, celebrations and disappointments, joys and sorrows, hopes and doubts.

But even when you feel very distant from God, remember that God is never distant from you. When you sincerely seek His presence, He will touch your heart, calm your fears, and restore our soul.

Mark it down. God never turns away the honest seeker. Go to God with your questions. You may not find all the answers, but in finding God, you know the One who does.

Max Lucado

&> Doubt is not always a sign that a man is wrong; it may be a sign that he is thinking.

Oswald Chambers

&> Doubting may temporarily disturb but will not permanently destroy your faith in Christ.

Charles Swindoll

&> Faith has no value of its own; it has value only as it connects us with Him. It is a trick of Satan to get us occupied with examining our faith instead of resting in the Faithful One.

Vance Havner

&> There is a difference between doubt and unbelief. Doubt is a matter of mind: we cannot understand what God is doing or why He is doing it. Unbelief is a matter of will: we refuse to believe God's Word and obey what He tells us to do.

Warren Wiersbe

&ඏ In our constant struggle to believe, we are likely to overlook the simple fact that a bit of healthy disbelief is sometimes as needful as faith to the welfare of our souls.

A. W. Tozer

&ඏ The Holy Spirit is no skeptic, and the things he has written in our hearts are not doubts or opinions but assertions—surer and more certain than sense or life itself.

Martin Luther

&ඏ A VERSE AND A PRAYER ඏ

In my distress I prayed to the LORD,
and the LORD answered me and rescued me.
The LORD is for me, so I will not be afraid.
Psalm 118:5-6 NLT

Dear God, sometimes this world can be a puzzling place, filled with uncertainty and doubt. When I am unsure of my next step, keep me mindful that You are always near and that You can overcome any challenge. Give me faith, Father, and let me remember always that with Your love and Your power, I can live courageously and faithfully today and every day. ~Amen

DISCOVERING THE POWER OF OPTIMISM

*For God has not given us a spirit of fearfulness,
but one of power, love, and sound judgment.*
2 Timothy 1:7 HCSB

A re you an optimistic, hopeful, enthusiastic Christian? You should be. After all, as a believer, you have every reason to be optimistic about life here on earth and life eternal.

As C. H. Spurgeon observed, "Our hope in Christ for the future is the mainstream of our joy." But sometimes, you may find yourself pulled down by the inevitable demands and worries of life-here-on-earth. If you find yourself discouraged, exhausted, or both, then it's time to take your concerns to God. When you do, He will lift your spirits and renew your strength.

Today, make this promise to yourself and keep it: vow to be a hope-filled Christian. Think optimistically about your life, your work, your family, and your future. Trust your hopes not your fears. Take time to celebrate God's glorious creation. And then, when you've filled your heart with hope and gladness, share your optimism with others. They'll be better for it, and so will you.

so The people whom I have seen succeed best in life have always been cheerful and hopeful people who went about their business with a smile on their faces.

Charles Kingsley

so The essence of optimism is that it takes no account of the present, but it is a source of inspiration, of vitality, and of hope. Where others have resigned, it enables a man to hold his head high, to claim the future for himself, and not abandon it to his enemy.

Dietrich Bonhoeffer

so Make the least of all that goes and the most of all that comes. Don't regret what is past. Cherish what you have. Look forward to all that is to come. And most important of all, rely moment by moment on Jesus Christ.

Gigi Graham Tchividjian

so Keep your feet on the ground, but let your heart soar as high as it will. Refuse to be average or to surrender to the chill of your spiritual environment.

A. W. Tozer

⁚ Oh, remember this: There is never a time when we may not hope in God. Whatever our necessities, however great our difficulties, and though to all appearance help is impossible, yet our business is to hope in God, and it will be found that it is not in vain.

George Mueller

⁚ Never yield to gloomy anticipation. Place your hope and confidence in God. He has no record of failure.

Mrs. Charles E. Cowman

⁚ A VERSE AND A PRAYER ₞

But as for me, I will always have hope;
I will praise you more and more.

Psalm 71:14 NIV

Lord, give me faith, optimism, and hope. Let me expect the best from You, and let me look for the best in others. Let me trust You, Lord, to direct my life. And, let me be Your faithful, hopeful, optimistic servant every day that I live. ~Amen

BECOMING YOUR OWN PERSON; USING YOUR OWN GIFTS

When I was a child, I spoke and thought
and reasoned as a child does.
But when I grew up, I put away childish things.
1 Corinthians 13:11 NLT

When God made you, He equipped you with an array of talents and abilities that are uniquely yours. It's up to you to discover those talents and to use them, but sometimes the world will encourage you to do otherwise. At times, our society will attempt to cubbyhole you, to standardize you, and to make you fit into a particular, preformed mold. Perhaps God has other plans.

Have you found something in this life that you're passionate about? Something that inspires you to jump out of bed in the morning and hit the ground running? And does your work honor the Creator by making His world a better place? If so, congratulations: you're using your gifts well.

Sometimes, because you're a fallible human being, you may become so wrapped up in meeting *society's* expectations that you fail to focus on *God's* expectations. To do so is a mistake of major proportions—don't make it. Instead, seek God's guidance as you focus your energies on becoming the best "you" that you can possibly be.

What's the best way to thank God for the gifts that He has given you? By using them. And, you might as well start using them today.

∞ In the great orchestra we call life, you have an instrument and a song, and you owe it to God to play them both sublimely.

Max Lucado

∞ I've never met anyone who became instantly mature. It's a painstaking process that God takes us through, and it includes such things as waiting, failing, losing, and being misunderstood—each calling for extra doses of perseverance.

Charles Swindoll

∞ Being a Christian means accepting the terms of creation, accepting God as our Maker and Redeemer, and growing day by day into an increasingly glorious creature in Christ, developing joy, experiencing love, maturing in peace.

Eugene Peterson

∞ A Christian is never in a state of completion but always in the process of becoming.

Martin Luther

୭ Grass that is here today and gone tomorrow does not require much time to mature. A big oak tree that lasts for generations requires much more time to grow and mature. God is concerned about your life through eternity. Allow Him to take all the time He needs to shape you for His purposes. Larger assignments will require longer periods of preparation.

Henry Blackaby

୭ God loves us the way we are, but He loves us too much to leave us that way.

Leighton Ford

୭ A VERSE AND A PRAYER ৎ

I will instruct you and teach you in the way you should go;
I will counsel you and watch over you.

Psalm 32:8 NIV

Thank You, Lord, that I am not yet what I am to become. The Holy Scripture tells me that You are at work in my life, continuing to help me grow and to mature in the faith. Show me Your wisdom, Father, and let me live according to Your Word and Your will. ~Amen

PURPOSE THROUGH SERVICE

> *But whoever desires to become great among you,*
> *let him be your servant. And whoever desires to be*
> *first among you, let him be your slave—just as*
> *the Son of Man did not come to be served, but to serve,*
> *and to give His life a ransom for many."*
> Matthew 20:26-28 NKJV

J esus teaches that the most esteemed men and women are not the self-congratulatory leaders of society but are instead the humblest of servants. But, as weak human beings, we sometimes fall short as we seek to puff ourselves up and glorify our own accomplishments. To do so is wrong.

Today, as you plan for the next phase of your life's journey, you may feel the temptation to build yourself up in the eyes of your neighbors. Resist that temptation. Instead, serve your neighbors quietly and without fanfare. Find a need and fill it . . . humbly. Lend a helping hand and share a word of kindness . . . anonymously. This is God's way.

As a humble servant, you will glorify yourself not before men but before God, and that's what God intends. After all, earthly glory is fleeting: here today and all too soon gone. But, heavenly glory endures throughout eternity. So, the choice is yours: Either you can lift yourself up here on earth and be humbled in heaven or vice versa. Choose vice versa.

Service is the pathway to real significance.

Rick Warren

Christianity, in its purest form, is nothing more than seeing Jesus. Christian service, in its purest form, is nothing more than imitating Him who we see. To see His majesty and to imitate Him: that is the sum of Christianity.

Max Lucado

No life can surpass that of a man who quietly continues to serve God in the place where Providence has placed him.

C. H. Spurgeon

Before the judgment seat of Christ, my service will not be judged by how much I have done but by how much of me there is in it.

A. W. Tozer

God wants us to serve Him with a willing spirit, one that would choose no other way.

Beth M

ℵ In Jesus, the service of God and the service of the least of the brethren were one.

Dietrich Bonhoeffer

ℵ Determine to abide in Jesus wherever you are placed.

Oswald Chambers

ℵ A VERSE AND A PRAYER ଔ

Your attitude should be the same as that of Christ Jesus . . .
taking the very nature of a servant.

Philippians 2:5,7 NIV

Lord, You have promised me a life of abundance and joy through Your Son Jesus. Thank You, Lord, for Your blessings, and guide me according to Your will, so that I might be a worthy servant in all that I say and do, this day and every day. ~Amen

PRAYING ON PURPOSE FOR PURPOSE

Whatever you ask for in prayer,
believe that you have received it,
and it will be yours.
Mark 11:24 NIV

Have you fervently asked God for His guidance in every aspect of your life? If so, then you're continually inviting your Creator to reveal Himself in a variety of ways. As a follower of Christ, you must do no less.

Jesus made it clear to His disciples: they should pray always. So should we. Genuine, heartfelt prayer produces powerful changes in us *and* in our world. When we lift our hearts to our Father in heaven, we open ourselves to a never-ending source of divine wisdom and infinite love.

Do you have questions about your future that you simply can't answer? Ask for the guidance of your Heavenly Father. Do you sincerely seek to know God's purpose for your life? Then ask Him for direction—and *keep* asking Him every day that you live. Whatever your need, no matter how great or small, pray about it and never lose hope. God is not just near; He is here, and He's ready to talk with you. Now!

℠ We must understand that the first and chief thing—for everyone who would do the work of Jesus—is to believe, and in doing so, to become linked to Him, the Almighty One . . . and then, to pray the prayer of faith in His name.

Andrew Murray

℠ As I quietly abide in You and let Your life flow into me, what freedom it is to know that the Father does not see my threadbare patience or insufficient trust, rather only Your patience, Lord, and Your confidence that the Father has everything in hand. In Your faith I thank You right now for a more glorious answer to my prayer than I can imagine. Amen.

Catherine Marshall

℠ Four things let us ever keep in mind: God hears prayer, God heeds prayer, God answers prayer, and God delivers by prayer.

E. M. Bounds

℠ God wants to remind us that nothing on earth or in hell can ultimately stand against the man or the woman who calls on the name of the Lord!

Jim Cymbala

❧ The Scriptures teach that we can pray effectively for one another and that such a petition "availeth much." I believe God honors and answers this kind of intercessory prayer.

James Dobson

❧ The manifold rewards of a serious, consistent prayer life demonstrate clearly that time with our Lord should be our first priority.

Shirley Dobson

❧ A VERSE AND A PRAYER ❧

The earnest prayer of a righteous person has great power and wonderful results.

James 5:16 NLT

Dear Lord, I will open my heart to You. I will take my concerns, my fears, my plans, and my hopes to You in prayer. And, then, I will trust the answers that You give. You are my loving Father, and I will accept Your will for my life today and every day that I live. ~Amen

CHANGES, CHANGES, AND MORE CHANGES

> There is a time for everything,
> and a season for every activity under heaven.
>
> *Ecclesiastes* 3:1 NIV

G raduation is a time of transition. Everything around you may seem to be in a state of flux, and you may be required to make lots of adjustments. If all these events have left your head spinning and your heart pounding, don't worry: although the world is in a state of constant change, God is not.

Even if the changes in your life are unfolding at a furious pace, you can be comforted in the knowledge that your Heavenly Father is the rock that cannot be shaken. His Word promises, "I am the LORD, I do not change" (Malachi 3:6 NKJV).

As a recent graduate, you're facing an exciting time, a time filled with possibilities and opportunities. But, if your transition to the next phase of life proves difficult, don't worry: God is far bigger than any challenge you may face.

Remember that "Jesus Christ is the same yesterday, today, and forever" (Hebrews 13:8 NKJV). And rest assured: It is precisely because your Savior *does not change* that you can face the transitions of life with courage for today and hope for tomorrow.

&co When we are young, change is a treat, but as we grow older, change becomes a threat. But when Jesus Christ is in control of your life, you need never fear change or decay.

Warren Wiersbe

&co When you're through changing, you're through!

John Maxwell

&co Sometimes your medicine bottle says, "Shake well before using." That is what God has to do with some of His people. He has to shake them well before they are usable.

Vance Havner

&co The moment you wake up each morning, all your wishes and hopes for the day rush at you like wild animals. And the first job each morning consists in shoving it all back; in listening to that other voice, taking that other point of view, letting that other, larger, stronger, quieter life coming flowing in.

C. S. Lewis

ℂ A God wise enough to create me and the world I live in is wise enough to watch out for me.

Philip Yancey

ℂ He goes before us, follows behind us, and hems us safe inside the realm of His protection.

Beth Moore

ℂ A VERSE AND A PRAYER ℂ

Be strong and courageous. Do not be terrified;
do not be discouraged, for the LORD your God
will be with you wherever you go.

Joshua 1:9 NIV

Dear Lord, our world changes, but You are unchanging. When I face challenges that leave me discouraged or fearful, I will turn to You for strength and assurance. Let my trust in You—like Your love for me—be unchanging and everlasting. ~Amen

HELPING FRIENDS THROUGH TOUGH TIMES

A friend loves you all the time,
and a brother helps in time of trouble.

Proverbs 17:17 NCV

On occasion, all of us face tough times. But, when we encounter setbacks, God stands ready to protect us. Psalm 147 promises, "He heals the brokenhearted, and binds their wounds" (v. 3 NASB). When we are troubled, we can call upon Him, and—in His own time and according to His own plan—He will heal us.

Sometimes, of course, it is not us, but instead our friends, who face adversity. When friends or family members encounter troubling circumstances, our mission is simple: We must assist in any way we can, either with an encouraging word, a helping hand, or a heartfelt prayer.

The English clergyman Charles Kingsley had practical advice for Christians of every generation. He advised, "Make it a rule, and pray to God to help you to keep it, never, if possible, to lie down at night without being able to say: 'I have made one human being at least a little wiser, or a little happier, or at least a little better this day.'" Amen to that . . . especially when times are tough.

℺ A Christian is someone who shares the sufferings of God in the world.

Dietrich Bonhoeffer

℺ The crown of victory is promised only to those who engage in the struggle.

St. Augustine

℺ Adversity stirs us up and causes us to look at life differently. We are forced to deal with things on a deeper level. Nothing causes "self" to cave in like suffering. And once our religious facade begins to wear thin, God moves in and begins teaching us what real Christlikeness is about.

Charles Swindoll

℺ Underneath each trouble there is a faithful purpose.

C. H. Spurgeon

℺ Man's adversity is God's opportunity.

Matthew Henry

ဢ Discouraged people don't need critics. They hurt enough already. They don't need more guilt or piled-on distress. They need encouragement. They need a refuge, a willing, caring, available someone.

Charles Swindoll

ဢ No journey is complete that does not lead through some dark valleys. We can properly comfort others only with the comfort we ourselves have been given by God.

Vance Havner

ဢ A VERSE AND A PRAYER ের

In this world you will have trouble.
But take heart! I have overcome the world.

John 16:33 NIV

Dear Lord, when I am troubled, You comfort me. When I am discouraged, You lift me up. Whatever my circumstances, Lord, I will trust Your plan for my life. And, when my family and friends are troubled, I will remind them of Your love, Your wisdom, and Your grace. ~Amen

PURPOSEFUL WORSHIP, PURPOSEFUL PRAISE

All the earth shall worship You
And sing praises to You;
They shall sing praises to Your name.
Psalm 66:4 NKJV

All of humanity is engaged in worship. The question is not *whether* we worship but *what* we worship. Wise men and women choose to worship God. When they do, they are blessed with a plentiful harvest of joy, peace, and abundance. Other people choose to distance themselves from God by foolishly worshiping things that are intended to bring *personal* gratification not *spiritual* gratification. Such choices often have tragic consequences.

If we place our love for material possessions above our love for God—or if we yield to the countless temptations of this world—we find ourselves engaged in a struggle between good and evil, a clash between God and Satan. Our responses to these struggles have implications that echo throughout our families and throughout our communities.

How can we ensure that we cast our lot with God? We do so, in part, by the practice of regular, purposeful worship in the company of fellow believers. When we worship God faithfully and fervently, we are blessed. When we fail to worship God, for whatever reason, we forfeit the spiritual gifts that He intends for us.

We must worship our Heavenly Father not just with our words but also with deeds. We must honor Him, praise Him, and obey Him. As we seek to find purpose and meaning for our lives, we must first seek *His* purpose and *His* will. For believers, God comes first. Period.

◈ I am of the opinion that we should not be concerned about working for God until we have learned the meaning and delight of worshipping Him.

A. W. Tozer

◈ God asks that we worship Him with our concentrated minds as well as with our wills and emotions. A divided and scattered mind is not effective.

Catherine Marshall

◈ When we obey the command to praise God in worship, our deep, essential need to be in relationship with God is nurtured.

Eugene Peterson

◈ Praise Him! Praise Him! Tell of His excellent greatness. Praise Him! Praise Him! Ever in joyful song!

Fanny Crosby

◈ It is impossible to worship God and remain unchanged.

Henry Blackaby

❧ The fact that we were created to enjoy God and to worship Him forever is etched upon our souls.

Jim Cymbala

❧ Worship is a voluntary act of gratitude offered by the saved to the Savior, by the healed to the Healer, and by the delivered to the Deliverer.

Max Lucado

❧ A VERSE AND A PRAYER ❧

O come, let us sing unto the LORD: let us make
a joyful noise to the rock of our salvation.
Let us come before his presence with thanksgiving,
and make a joyful noise unto him with psalms.

Psalm 95:1-2 KJV

When I worship You, Dear Lord, You set my path—and my heart—straight. Let this day and every day be a time of worship. Whether I am in Your house or simply going about my daily activities, let me worship You, not only with words and deeds but also with my heart. In the quiet moments of the day, I will praise You for creating me, loving me, guiding me, and saving me. ~Amen

A TIME TO GROW

> *But grow in the special favor and knowledge of our Lord and Savior Jesus Christ. To him be all glory and honor, both now and forevermore. Amen.*
>
> 2 Peter 3:18 NLT

Graduation is an important milestone in your education, but the end of the school year *should not* mark the end of your intellectual growth. Hopefully, you will keep learning every day that you live. And so it is with *spiritual* growth: the journey toward spiritual maturity should last a lifetime. As Christians, we can and should continue to grow in the love and the knowledge of our Savior as long as we live.

Norman Vincent Peale had simple advice for believers of all ages. Dr. Peale said, "Ask the God who made you to keep remaking you." That advice, of course, is perfectly sound but too often ignored.

When we cease to grow, either emotionally or spiritually, we do ourselves and our families a profound disservice. But, if we study God's Word, if we obey His commandments, and if we live in the center of His will, we will not be "stagnant" believers; we will, instead, be growing Christians . . . and that's exactly what God wants for our lives.

In those quiet moments when we open our hearts to God, the Creator who made us keeps remaking us. He gives us direction, perspective, wisdom, and courage. And, the appropriate moment to accept His spiritual gifts is always this one.

› God's goal is that we move toward maturity—all our past failures and faults notwithstanding.

Charles Swindoll

› God gives us a compass and a Book of promises and principles—the Bible—and lets us make our decisions day by day as we sense the leading of His Spirit. This is how we grow.

Warren Wiersbe

› You are either becoming more like Christ every day or you're becoming less like Him. There is no neutral position in the Lord.

Stormie Omartian

› Salvation is the process that's done, that's secure, that no one can take away from you. Sanctification is the lifelong process of being changed from one degree of glory to the next, growing in Christ, putting away the old, taking on the new.

Max Lucado

› Spiritual growth consists most in the growth of the root, which is out of sight.

Matthew Henry

๑ If you lack knowledge, go to school. If you lack wisdom, get on your knees.

Vance Havner

๑ Knowledge can be found in books or in school. Wisdom, on the other hand, starts with God . . . and ends there.

Marie T. Freeman

๑ A VERSE AND A PRAYER ๛

*Happy is the person who finds wisdom
and gains understanding.*

Proverbs 3:13 NLT

Dear Lord, when I open myself to You, I am blessed. Let me accept Your love and Your wisdom, Father. Show me Your way, and deliver me from the painful mistakes that I make when I stray from Your commandments. Let me live according to Your Word, and let me grow in my faith every day that I live. ~Amen

ATTITUDE ADJUSTMENTS

Finally brothers, whatever is true, whatever is honorable, whatever is just, whatever is pure, whatever is lovely, whatever is commendable—if there is any moral excellence and if there is any praise—dwell on these things.

Philippians 4:8 HCSB

Thoughts are intensely powerful things. Our thoughts have the power to lift us up or drag us down; they have the power to energize us or deplete us, to inspire us to greater accomplishments or to make those accomplishments impossible.

How will you direct your thoughts today? Will you obey the words of Philippians 4:8 by dwelling upon those things that are honorable, true, and worthy of praise? Or will you allow your thoughts to be hijacked by the negativity that seems to dominate our troubled world?

Are you fearful, angry, bored, or worried? Are you so preoccupied with the concerns of this day that you fail to thank God for the promise of eternity? Are you confused, bitter, or pessimistic? If so, God wants to have a little talk with you.

God intends that you experience joy and abundance, but He will not force His joy upon you; you must claim it for yourself. It's up to you to celebrate the life that God has given you by focusing your mind upon "whatever is of good repute." Today, spend more time thinking about your blessings and less time fretting about your hardships. Then, take time to thank the Giver of all things good for gifts that are, in truth, far too numerous to count.

ဢ I could go through this day oblivious to the miracles all around me, or I could tune in and "enjoy."

Gloria Gaither

ဢ I have witnessed many attitudes make a positive turnaround through prayer.

John Maxwell

ဢ Outlook determines outcome and attitude determines action.

Warren Wiersbe

ဢ Your attitude, not your aptitude, will determine your altitude.

Zig Ziglar

ဢ The world's sewage system threatens to contaminate the stream of Christian thought. Is the world shaping your mind, or is Christ?

Billy Graham

ℹ Be assured, my dear friend, that it is no joy to God in seeing you with a dreary countenance.

C. H. Spurgeon

ℹ God is good, and heaven is forever. And if those two facts don't cheer you up, nothing will.

Marie T. Freeman

ℹ A VERSE AND A PRAYER ℺

The cheerful heart has a continual feast.

Proverbs 15:15 NIV

Lord, I pray for an attitude that is Christlike. Whatever my circumstances, whether good or bad, triumphal or tragic, let my response reflect a God-honoring attitude of optimism, faith, and love for You. ~Amen

TRUSTING GOD'S PROMISES

Trust in the LORD with all your heart, and lean not on your own understanding; in all your ways acknowledge Him, and He shall direct your paths.

Proverbs 3:5-6 NKJV

Now that you've graduated, you can put your books aside . . . except for *The Book*: God's Holy Word. The Bible is a roadmap for life here on earth and for life eternal; it should be *the* map for you.

As believers, we must study the Bible daily and meditate upon its meaning for our lives. Otherwise, we deprive ourselves of a priceless gift from our Creator. God's Holy Word is, indeed, a transforming, life-changing, one-of-a-kind treasure. A passing acquaintance with the Good Book is insufficient for Christians who seek to obey God's Word and to understand His will.

Jonathan Edwards advised, "Be assiduous in reading the Holy Scriptures. This is the fountain whence all knowledge in divinity must be derived. Therefore let not this treasure lie by you neglected."

God's Holy Word is, indeed, a priceless, one-of-a-kind treasure. Handle it with care, but more importantly, handle it every day.

🔊 The promises of Scripture are not mere pious hopes or sanctified guesses. They are more than sentimental words to be printed on decorated cards for Sunday School children. They are eternal verities. They are true. There is no perhaps about them.

Peter Marshall

🔊 The stars may fall, but God's promises will stand and be fulfilled.

J. I. Packer

🔊 Brother, is your faith looking upward today? Trust in the promise of the Savior. Sister, is the light shining bright on your way? Trust in the promise of thy Lord.

Fanny Crosby

🔊 We have ample evidence that the Lord is able to guide. The promises cover every imaginable situation. All we need to do is to take the hand He stretches out.

Elisabeth Elliot

🔊 God does not give us everything we want, but He does fulfill all His promises as He leads us along the best and straightest paths to Himself.

Dietrich Bonhoeffer

so We never prize the precious words of promise until we are placed in conditions in which their suitability and sweetness are manifested.

C. H. Spurgeon

so In Biblical worship you do not find the repetition of a phrase; instead, you find the worshipers rehearsing the character of God and His ways, reminding Him of His faithfulness and His wonderful promises.

Kay Arthur

so A VERSE AND A PRAYER cs

Your word is a lamp to my feet and a light to my path.

Psalm 119:105 NKJV

Lord, You have promised that You will provide for my needs, and I trust that promise. But sometimes, because of my imperfect faith, I fall prey to worry and doubt. Today, give me the courage to trust You completely. You are my protector, dear Lord; let me praise You, let me love You, and let me trust in the perfect wisdom of Your plan. ~Amen

DOING WHAT'S RIGHT

*Blessed are those who hunger and thirst for righteousness,
for they shall be filled.*

Matthew 5:6 NKJV

Oswald Chambers, the author of the Christian classic devotional text *My Utmost for His Highest*, advised, "Never support an experience which does not have God as its source and faith in God as its result." These words serve as a powerful reminder that, as Christians, we are called to walk with God and obey His commandments. But, we live in a world that presents us with countless temptations to stray far from God's path. We Christians, when confronted with sin, have clear instructions: Walk—or better yet run—in the opposite direction.

When we seek righteousness in our own lives—and when we seek the companionship of those who do likewise—we reap the spiritual rewards that God intends for our lives. When we live righteously and according to God's commandments, He blesses us in ways that we cannot fully understand.

Today, as you consider the exciting possibilities of life-after-graduation, make yourself this promise: Support only those activities that further God's kingdom and your own spiritual growth. Be an example of righteous living to your friends, to your neighbors, and to your family. Then, prepare to reap the blessings that God has promised to all those who live according to His will and His Word.

🔊 It may be said without qualification that every man is as holy and as full of the Spirit as he wants to be. He may not be as full as he wishes he were, but he is most certainly as full as he wants to be.

A. W. Tozer

🔊 What is God looking for? He is looking for men and women whose hearts are completely His.

Charles Swindoll

🔊 We must appropriate the tender mercy of God every day after conversion, or problems quickly develop. We need His grace daily in order to live a righteous life.

Jim Cymbala

🔊 It is quite true to say, "I can't live a holy life," but you can decide to let Jesus make you holy.

Oswald Chambers

🔊 Learning God's truth and getting it into our heads is one thing, but *living* God's truth and getting it into our characters is quite something else.

Warren Wiersbe

🔊 Holiness isn't in a style of dress. It's not a matter of rules and regulations. It's a way of life that emanates quietness and rest, joy in family, shared pleasures with friends, the help of a neighbor—and the hope of a Savior.

Joni Eareckson Tada

🔊 Let God use times of waiting to mold and shape your character. Let God use those times to purify your life and make you into a clean vessel for His service.

Henry Blackaby and Claude King

🔊 A VERSE AND A PRAYER ◌

Blessed is every one who fears the Lord,
who walks in His ways.

Psalm 128:1 NKJV

Lord, let me be honest and good, patient and kind, faithful to You and loving to others . . . now and forever. ~Amen

TRUST FOR TOMORROW

> *For the LORD God is our light and our protector.*
> *He gives us grace and glory. No good thing will the LORD*
> *withhold from those who do what is right. O LORD Almighty,*
> *happy are those who trust in you.*
>
> *Psalm 84:11-12 NLT*

Because we are saved by a risen Christ, we can have hope for the future, no matter how troublesome our present circumstances may seem. After all, God has promised that we are His throughout eternity. And, He has told us that we must place our hopes in Him.

Of course, we will face disappointments and failures while we are here on earth, but these are only temporary defeats. Of course, this world can be a place of trials and tribulations, but when we place our trust in the Giver of all things good, we are secure. God has promised us peace, joy, and eternal life. And God keeps His promises today, tomorrow, and forever.

Are you willing to place your future in the hands of a loving and all-knowing God? Do you trust in the ultimate goodness of His plan for your life? Will you face today's challenges with optimism and hope? You should. After all, God created you for a very important purpose: *His* purpose. And you still have important work to do: *His* work.

Today, as you live in the present and look to the future, remember that God has a plan for you. Act—and believe—accordingly.

℃ Never be afraid to trust an unknown future to an all-knowing God.

Corrie ten Boom

℃ To know God as He really is—in His essential nature and character—is to arrive at a citadel of peace that circumstances may storm, but can never capture.

Catherine Marshall

℃ Fear lurks in the shadows of every area of life. The future may look very threatening. Jesus says, "Stop being afraid. Trust me!"

Charles Swindoll

℃ Either we are adrift in chaos or we are individuals, created, loved, upheld and placed purposefully, exactly where we are. Can you believe that? Can you trust God for that?

Elisabeth Elliot

℃ When we are in a situation where Jesus is all we have, we soon discover he is all we really need.

Gigi Graham Tchividjian

୨୦ Mary could not have dreamed all that would result from her faithful obedience. Likewise, you cannot possibly imagine all that God has in store for you when you trust Him.

Henry Blackaby

୨୦ God's help is near and always available, but it is only given to those who seek it.

Max Lucado

୨୦ A VERSE AND A PRAYER ୦ଽ

I lift up my eyes to the hills—where does my help come from?
My help comes from the LORD,
the Maker of heaven and earth.

Psalm 121:1-2 NIV

Dear Lord, as I look to the future, I will place my trust in You. If I become discouraged, I will turn to You. If I am afraid, I will seek strength in You. You are my Father, and I will place my hope, my trust, and my faith in You.
~Amen

STRENGTH
FOR THE
JOURNEY

The LORD is my shepherd; I shall not want.
He makes me to lie down in green pastures;
He leads me beside the still waters. He restores my soul.

Psalm 23:1-3 NKJV

God is a never-ending source of strength and courage when we call upon Him. When we are weary, He gives us strength. When we see no hope, God reminds us of His promises. When we grieve, God wipes away our tears.

Do you feel burdened by today's responsibilities? Do you feel pressured by the ever-increasing demands of 21st-century life? Then turn your concerns and your prayers over to God. He knows your needs, and He has promised to meet those needs. Whatever your circumstances, God will protect you and care for you *if* you allow Him to preside over your life.

Today, invite God into your heart and allow Him to renew your spirits. When you trust Him and Him alone, He will never fail you.

Life after graduation can be challenging, but fear not. God loves you, and He will protect you. Whatever your challenge, God can handle it. Let Him.

⃠ And in truth, if we only knew it, our chief fitness is our utter helplessness. His strength is made perfect not in our strength but in our weakness. Our strength is only a hindrance.

Hannah Whitall Smith

⃠ Our Lord never drew power from Himself; He drew it always from His Father.

Oswald Chambers

⃠ God walks with us. He scoops us up in His arms or simply sits with us in silent strength until we cannot avoid the awesome recognition that yes, even now, He is here.

Gloria Gaither

⃠ One with God is a majority.

Billy Graham

⃠ Worry does not empty tomorrow of its sorrow; it empties today of its strength.

Corrie ten Boom

So Jesus is not a strong man making men and women who gather around Him weak. He is the Strong creating the strong.

E. Stanley Jones

So Notice what Jesus had to say concerning those who have wearied themselves by trying to do things in their own strength: "Come to me, all you who labor and are heavy laden, and I will give you rest."

Henry Blackaby and Claude King

So A VERSE AND A PRAYER ca

I can do all things through Christ who strengthens me.
Philippians 4:13 NKJV

Lord, You have promised never to leave me or forsake me. You are always with me, protecting me and encouraging me. Whatever this day may bring, I thank You for Your love and for Your strength. Let me lean upon You, Father, this day and forever. ~Amen

TIME FOR GOD

Be still, and know that I am God.

Psalm 46:10 NKJV

The words are as familiar as they are true: "First things first." But sometimes, in this busy world, placing first things first can be difficult indeed. Why? Because so many people are expecting so many things from us! That's why it is vitally important that we spend time with the One who can help us prioritize our days *and* our lives.

Today and every day, you should put first things first by prioritizing your life according to God. First and foremost, you should seek His will; you should obey His commandments; and you should trust His promises. Then, you can face each day with the assurance that the same God who created our universe out of nothingness can help you place first things first in your own life.

Do you have questions you can't answer? Are you genuinely seeking to understand God's plan for your life? If so, turn your concerns over to God—quietly, prayerfully, earnestly, and often. Then listen for His answers . . . and trust the answers that He gives.

⁣ The manifold rewards of a serious, consistent prayer life demonstrate clearly that time with our Lord should be our first priority.

Shirley Dobson

⁣ That is the source of Jeremiah's living persistence, his creative constancy. He was up before the sun, listening to God's word. Rising early, he was quiet and attentive before his Lord. Long before the yelling started, the mocking, the complaining, there was this centering, discovering, exploring time with God.

Eugene Peterson

⁣ As we find that it is not easy to persevere in this being "alone with God," we begin to realize that it is because we are not "wholly for God." God has a right to demand that He should have us completely for Himself.

Andrew Murray

⁣ Quietude, which some men cannot abide because it reveals their inward poverty, is as a palace of cedar to the wise, for along its hallowed courts, the King in His beauty deigns to walk.

C. H. Spurgeon

🔊 Make a plan now to keep a daily appointment with God. The enemy is going to tell you to set it aside, but you must carve out the time. If you're too busy to meet with the Lord, friend, then you are simply too busy.

Charles Swindoll

🔊 We all need to make time for God. Even Jesus made time to be alone with the Father.

Kay Arthur

🔊 A VERSE AND A PRAYER ൠ

The counsel of the LORD stands forever,
the plans of His heart to all generations.

Psalm 33:11 NKJV

Lord, Your Holy Word is a light unto the world; let me study it, trust it, and share it with all who cross my path. Let me discover You, Father, in the quiet moments of the day. And, in all that I say and do, help me to be a worthy witness as I share the Good News of Your perfect Son and Your perfect Word. ~Amen

WALKING HUMBLY

But he who is greatest among you shall be your servant.
And whoever exalts himself will be humbled,
and he who humbles himself will be exalted.

Matthew 23:11-12 NLT

We have heard the phrase on countless occasions: "He's a self-made man." In truth, none of us are self-made. We all owe countless debts that we can never repay. Our first debt, of course, is to our Father in heaven—Who has given us everything that we are and will ever be—and to His Son Who sacrificed His own life so that we might live eternally. We are also indebted to ancestors, parents, teachers, friends, spouses, family members, fellow believers . . . and the list goes on.

As Christians, we have a profound reason to be humble: We have been refashioned and saved by Jesus Christ, and that salvation came not because of our own good works but because of God's grace. Thus, we are not "self-made"; we are "God-made"; and "Christ-saved." How, then, can we be boastful? The answer, of course, is that, if we are honest with ourselves and with our God, we simply can't be boastful . . . we must, instead, be eternally grateful and exceedingly humble.

Humility is not, in most cases, a naturally-occurring human trait. Most of us, it seems, are more than willing to stick out our chests and say, "Look at me; I did that!" But in our better moments, in the quiet moments when we search the depths of our own hearts, we know better. Whatever "it" is, God did that. And He deserves the credit.

‽ Humility is the exhibition of the spirit of Jesus Christ and is the touchstone of saintliness.

Oswald Chambers

‽ Humility is not thinking less of yourself; it is thinking of yourself less.

Rick Warren

‽ Do you wish to be great? Then begin by being humble. Do you desire to construct a vast and lofty fabric? Think first about the foundations of humility. The higher your structure is to be, the deeper must be its foundation.

St. Augustine

‽ God uses broken things: broken soil and broken clouds to produce grain; broken grain to produce bread; broken bread to feed our bodies. He wants our stubbornness broken into humble obedience.

Vance Havner

‽ Nothing sets a person so much out of the devil's reach as humility.

Jonathan Edwards

❧ God exalts humility. When God works in our lives, helping us to become humble, He gives us a permanent joy. Humility gives us a joy that cannot be taken away.

Max Lucado

❧ Seeking after God is a two-pronged endeavor. It requires not only humility to say, "God, I need you," but also a heart that desires a pure life that is pleasing to the Lord.

Jim Cymbala

❧ A VERSE AND A PRAYER ❧

The reward of humility and the fear of the LORD are riches, honor and life.

Proverbs 22:4 NASB

Heavenly Father, Jesus clothed Himself with humility when He chose to leave heaven and come to earth to live and die for us, His children. Jesus is my Master and my example. Clothe me with humility, Lord, so that I might be more like Your Son. ~Amen

WATCHING FOR SIGNS

> *But seek first the kingdom of God and His righteousness,*
> *and all these things shall be added to you.*
>
> Matthew 6:33 NKJV

God has plans for your life, and it's up to you to discover those plans. In fact, your entire life should be a mission of discovery as you watch carefully for His signs.

God is always present, and He is always trying to get His message through. If you seek to discover God's will for your life—and you should—then you will contemplate His Word and petition Him often through heartfelt prayer. Additionally, you will train yourself to be watchful for the way that God answers your prayers. Sometimes, His signs will be obvious; other times, they will be more subtle. In either case, you can discern God's will *if* you wait patiently with your eyes open wide and your heart open wider.

If you're struggling to find solutions to life's toughest questions, don't give up. Instead, keep searching for wisdom, starting with God's wisdom. Be watchful, be patient, and be faithful. On every step of your journey, trust your Heavenly Father to show you the way: His way. Then, look for the signs that He will most certainly provide. When you do, you'll discover the divine insight that only God can give.

There is nothing on earth that can satisfy our deepest longing. We long to see God. The leaves of life are rustling with the rumor that we will—and we won't be satisfied until we do.

Max Lucado

Joy is available to all who seek His riches. The key to joy is found in the person of Jesus Christ and in His will.

Kay Arthur

One of the most wonderful things about knowing God is that there's always so much more to know, so much more to discover. Just when we least expect it, He intrudes into our neat and tidy notions about who He is and how He works.

Joni Eareckson Tada

The main thing that God asks for is our attention.

Jim Cymbala

Jesus is the personal approach from the unseen God coming so near that He becomes inescapable. You don't have to find Him—you just have to consent to be found.

E. Stanley Jones

&so; Life's major pursuit is not knowing self but knowing God. Unless God is the major pursuit of our lives, all other pursuits are dead-end streets, including trying to know ourselves.

Charles Swindoll

&so; Thirsty hearts are those whose longings have been wakened by the touch of God within them.

A. W. Tozer

&so; A VERSE AND A PRAYER &cs;

Draw near to God, and He will draw near to you.

James 4:8 HCSB

Lord, let Your will be my will. When I am confused, give me maturity and wisdom. When I am worried, give me courage and strength. Let me be Your faithful servant, Father, always seeking Your guidance and Your will for my life. ~Amen

A JOYFUL JOURNEY

These things I have spoken to you,
that My joy may remain in you,
and that your joy may be full.
John 15:11 NKJV

Christ made it clear: He intends that His joy would become our joy. Yet sometimes, amid the inevitable hustle and bustle of life here on earth, we can forfeit—albeit temporarily—the joy of Christ as we wrestle with the challenges of daily living.

Jonathan Edwards, the 18th-century American clergyman, observed, "Christ is not only a remedy for your weariness and trouble, but He will give you an abundance of the contrary: joy and delight. They who come to Christ do not only come to a resting-place after they have been wandering in a wilderness, but they come to a banqueting-house where they may rest, and where they may feast. They may cease from their former troubles and toils, and they may enter upon a course of delights and spiritual joys."

If today your heart is burdened, open the door of your soul to Christ. He will give you peace and joy. And, if you already have the joy of Christ in your heart, share it freely, just as Christ freely shared His joy with you.

৯ According to Jesus, it is God's will that His children be filled with the joy of life.

Catherine Marshall

৯ The Christian should be an alleluia from head to foot!

St. Augustine

৯ All movements of discipleship arrive at a place where joy is experienced. Every step of assent toward God develops the capacity to enjoy. Not only is there, increasingly, more to be enjoyed; there is steadily the acquired ability to enjoy it.

Eugene Peterson

৯ A life of intimacy with God is characterized by joy.

Oswald Chambers

৯ If you're a thinking Christian, you will be a joyful Christian.

Marie T. Freeman

ↄ Christ is not only a remedy for your weariness and trouble, but He will give you an abundance of the contrary: joy and delight.

Jonathan Edwards

ↄ A VERSE AND A PRAYER Ⅎ

Enter his gates with thanksgiving; go into his courts
with praise. Give thanks to him and bless his name.
For the LORD is good. His unfailing love continues forever,
and his faithfulness continues to each generation.

Psalm 100:4-5 NLT

Dear Lord, You have given me so many blessings; let me celebrate Your gifts. Make me thankful, loving, responsible, and wise. I praise You, Father, for the gift of Your Son and for the priceless gift of salvation. Make me be a joyful Christian, a worthy example to others, and a dutiful servant to You this day and forever. ~Amen

AND FINALLY...

I have come that they may have life,
and that they may have it more abundantly.

John 10:10 NKJV

God sent His Son so that mankind might enjoy the abundant life that Jesus describes in the familiar words of John 10:10. But, God's gifts are not guaranteed; they must be claimed by those who choose to follow Christ. As you plan for life after graduation, you may be asking yourself, "What kind of life does God intend for me?" The answer can be found in God's promise of abundance: those who accept that promise and live according to God's commandments are eternally blessed.

Whether or not we accept God's abundance is, of course, up to each of us. When we entrust our hearts and our days to the One who created us, we experience God's peace through the grace and sacrifice of His Son. But, when we turn our thoughts and our energies away from God's commandments, we inevitably forfeit the earthly peace and spiritual abundance that might otherwise be ours.

so The Bible says that being a Christian is not only a great way to die, but it's also the best way to live.

Bill Hybels

so God is the Giver, and we are the receivers. And His richest gifts are bestowed not upon those who do the greatest things but upon those who accept His abundance and His grace.

Hannah Whitall Smith

so Oh! what a Savior, gracious to all, Oh! how His blessings round us fall, Gently to comfort, kindly to cheer, Sleeping or waking, God is near.

Fanny Crosby

so God proved His love on the cross. When Christ hung, and bled, and died, it was God saying to the world—I love you.

Billy Graham

so Christians are not citizens of earth trying to get to heaven, but citizens of heaven making their way through this world.

Vance Havner

⁊ When God blesses us, He expects us to use those blessings to bless the lives of others.

Jim Gallery

⁊ If you aren't serving, you're just existing because life is meant for ministry.

Rick Warren

⁊ A VERSE AND A PRAYER ☘

*Now this I say, he who sows sparingly will also
reap sparingly, and he who sows bountifully
will also reap bountifully.*

2 Corinthians 9:6 NASB

Father, thank You for the joyful, abundant life that is mine through Christ Jesus. Guide me according to Your will, and help me to be a worthy servant through all that I say and do. Give me courage, Lord, to claim the spiritual riches that You have promised, and lead me according to Your plan for my life, today and always. ~Amen